The Top 10 Bankruptcy Secrets Your Creditors Don't Want You to Know

William H Ridings Jr

Legal Disclaimer

Neither the publisher, the author nor the law firm assumes any responsibility for the use or misuse of information contained in this book. This is an educational book and not a means of extending legal advice. Having this book, owning it or reading it does not create an attorney-client privilege or legal relationship between the reader and the author. This book provides a general overview of the issues involving bankruptcy. The laws, case law, legislative policies and concepts discussed in the book, can change at any time. Procedures change and courts may change their opinions, or even interpret the law differently from each other. No book or web site can ever replace the sound advice from a lawyer in your own state. This book is intended for educational and informational purposes only.

Dedication

I want to thank my wife Linda for her support, help and love. This book would not have been possible without her. Thank you for believing and sharing life's successes and challenges with me. I look forward to growing old with you. Dream, take action, prosper.

Table of Contents

Dedication 3
Table of Contents 4
Introduction 7
Who Invented Bankruptcy? 9
What Leads to Bankruptcy? 10
The Startling Truth About Your Creditors 13
    What Your Creditors are Thinking 13
The Top 10 Secrets Your Creditors Don't Want YOU to Know 16
Secret #1: 20
Bankruptcy Can Eliminate Your Debts OR Help You Pay Them Off . 20
    Understanding the Two Types of Bankruptcy 20
    Success Story: Chapter 7 Bankruptcy 23
    Success Story: Chapter 13 Bankruptcy 23
Secret #2: 25
Filing Bankruptcy Will STOP the Debt Collection Calls 25
    Success Story: Stopping the Calls 26
Secret #3: 28
Bankruptcy Can STOP Foreclosure 28
    Delaying Foreclosure with the Automatic Stay 29
    Chapter 7 Bankruptcy and Foreclosure 30
    Chapter 13 Bankruptcy and Foreclosure 30
    Success Story: Stopping Foreclosure 31
Secret #4: 32
You Won't "Lose Everything" 32

A Fresh Start vs. A Head Start 32

Success Story: Getting a Fresh Start 33

Secret #5: 35

You Will Still Be Able to Purchase a Home or a Car 35

What About My Credit Score? 36

Success Story: Credit to Buy a Home 37

Success Story: Buying a Used Car 37

Secret #6: 38

You Don't Have to Be Out of Work to File Bankruptcy 38

Taking the Means Test 38

Success Story: Passing the Means Test 39

Secret #7: 41

Even High-Income Earners Can Qualify for Bankruptcy 41

What About Means Testing? 41

Success Story: High Income Earners File Chapter 13 Bankruptcy..42

Success Story: High Income Earners File Chapter 7 Bankruptcy....43

Success Story: Discharging Business Debts 43

Secret #8: 45

Credit Counselors are NOT Your Friends 45

What the U.S. Government Says About Credit Counselors and Bankruptcy 46

Success Story: Completing Required Credit Counseling in ONE Day 49

Secret #9: 50

You Can File Bankruptcy More Than Once 50

How Often Can You File Bankruptcy? 50

Changes to Automatic Stay on a Second Filing 51

Success Story: Filing Bankruptcy More Than Once 51

Secret #10: 53

You Don't Need an Attorney to File Bankruptcy 53

    Mistakes Often Made When Filing "Pro Se" 53

The Top 7 Reasons to Schedule a FREE Consultation with Ridings Law Firm 56

About the Author 57

    Contact Information: 58

Introduction

If you're like most of my clients, you're probably reading this book because you have bills you can't afford to pay. It's likely that collection agencies are calling you every week, if not every day. You may be experiencing stress in your relationships too. Because when finances are tight it seems to affect everything else. **If you're trying to decide whether bankruptcy is the right option for you and your family, you're in the right place.**

The first and most important step in deciding about bankruptcy is to understand what it can and cannot do for you. You'll learn exactly what you need to know as you read this book.

The second and equally important thing to know is the TRUTH about your creditors.

Your creditors want you to believe that your financial situation is "all your fault". They want you to believe that they are coming after you and that there is absolutely nothing you can do to stop them.

The truth is, there is plenty you *can* do to stop them.

But if you don't know what your rights are under the law, you will continue to be at the mercy of the creditors and collectors who mercilessly call you day after day until you're ready to do just about *anything* to make them stop.

I'm here to tell you...

You don't have to give in!

While it may be your responsibility to "pay up", it's also your responsibility to protect your family, meet their needs and look out for your own financial future. You don't have to let creditors manipulate you into giving them exactly what *they* want, regardless of whether *you* can afford it or not!

I'm about to share with you 10 Secrets that will help you take control of your financial future and get creditors off your back for good. If you're on the verge of bankruptcy...if you have creditors hounding you to pay bills you know there's *no way* you'll ever be able to pay off...then you're in luck. It's only good news from here on out!

Sincerely,

William H Ridings Jr

Who Invented Bankruptcy?

In ancient times, people who could not pay their debts were either put into debtors' prison or sold into slavery. Debtors were actually able to sell themselves in order to pay their debts. Members of their family and their own servants or slaves could also be sold or taken possession of by creditors. It was an awful situation to be in.

The concept of bankruptcy originated with the Old Testament. Moses references the Jubilee or Holy Year in which all debts would be eliminated and all debtors who had sold themselves into slavery to pay their debts would go free. Originally this Jubilee took place every 50 years (see Leviticus 25:10-13).

In Deuteronomy 15:1-2, Moses received a new law that increased the frequency of debt relief to every seven years. "At the end of every seven years you must cancel debts. This is how it is to be done: Every creditor shall cancel the loan he has made to his fellow Israelite. He shall not require payment from his fellow Israelite or brother, because the Lord's time for canceling debts has been proclaimed."

Our U.S. bankruptcy laws are based on the Mosaic Law in the Bible. Whether you're religious or not, you can benefit from today's legal release from debt.

While no one wants to declare bankruptcy, isn't is good to know that when your situation is truly out of control, you have the option to get a fresh start and have your debts forgiven?

What Leads to Bankruptcy?

According to USCourts.gov, 1,000,083 bankruptcies were filed during the 12 months ending June 30, 2014. Of these, 22,337 were filed in Missouri alone.[1]

So what leads over *one million* people to file bankruptcy?

According to Investopedia.com, the top five reasons people file bankruptcy are:[2]

1. **Medical Expenses.** According to a study conducted by Harvard and cited by Investopedia, 62% of bankruptcies were caused by medical expenses. And of those declaring bankruptcy, 78% had insurance. So it's not just the uninsured that end up in bankruptcy due to medical expenses.

2. **Job Loss.** When you lose your job, you lose your income. And unless you've built up a nice nest egg just in case something like this happens, you're bound to get behind on your bills. Another problem with unemployment is loss of health insurance. The cost of COBRA insurance alone can lead to an accumulation of debt that can be difficult to repay.

3. **Excess or Misuse of Credit.** How many days go by without you receiving a credit card offer in the mail? Not many. With the amount of credit card offers we receive, it's no wonder so many Americans have "too much credit". According to MyFico.com, "The typical consumer has access to

---

[1] http://www.uscourts.gov/Statistics/BankruptcyStatistics/2014-bankruptcy-filings.aspx
[2] http://www.investopedia.com/slide-show/top-5-reasons-why-people-go-bankrupt/

approximately $19,000 on all credit cards combined."[3] According to NerdWallet.com, the average indebted American carries a credit card balance of $15,607.[4]

4. **Divorce.** Divorce or separation can nearly double your living expenses. You're paying for two homes instead of one. You must provide furnishings for kids at both homes. Your transportation costs, if you have joint physical custody, increase. Dividing a household makes it harder than ever to make ends meet, especially if one or both spouses is unemployed or underemployed.

5. **Unexpected Expenses.** One family of five recently experienced an onslaught of expenses that could have pushed them over the edge financially:

    - The husband's car needed new tires.
    - They had to purchase a new air conditioning unit.
    - Their rental property had to be treated for a termite infestation.
    - A wind storm damaged a tree that required hundreds of dollars to be pruned.
    - Their dishwasher stopped working and had to be replaced

Unexpected expenses often lead to credit card debt when income isn't high enough to cover the required purchases. Then it's often all downhill from there.

---

[3] http://ficoforums.myfico.com/t5/Credit-Cards/AVERAGE-PERSONS-AVAILABLE-CREDIT/td-p/598392
[4] http://www.nerdwallet.com/blog/credit-card-data/average-credit-card-debt-household/

While you may find yourself deep in debt, upon thorough examination you may also decide that many of your expenses were necessary, unavoidable or contributed to by unforeseen circumstances.

While you are the one who spent the money, keep in mind that creditors are usually wrong when they try to tell you it's "ALL" your fault. If you've experienced any of the contributing life experiences mentioned above—medical expenses, job loss, excess credit, divorce, separation, or unexpected expenses—give yourself a break. Everyone experiences difficult times. And everyone, at one point or another, needs a fresh start.

Give yourself permission to start over if that's what you decide you truly need. That's what the law is designed to provide.

The Startling Truth About Your Creditors

You may be feeling terribly guilty...even kicking yourself with every negative thought you can muster about how you got yourself into this mess. But what do you think your creditors are thinking?

I'll tell you what they're thinking...

Your creditors *love* the fact that you can't pay your bills. They love collecting—or at least charging—late fees. They love increasing your interest rate because you've missed payments. And they love charging your new higher interest rate on your increasing balance *and* the late fees you've been racking up.

The fact of the matter is that the later you are, the more money they make in the long run.

What Your Creditors are Thinking

If you've been telling yourself that you should "be responsible" and "do the right thing" by paying off your bills, it's time to take a look at what your creditor are thinking about.

#1 Your creditors are celebrating. They're watching your mounting balances and they're throwing themselves a party because of all the money they're going to collect from you.

#2 They're thrilled to have do-gooders in debt to them. They love people like you who so desperately want to do the "right thing." They love you because they know you'll sacrifice just about anything—your family's welfare, your home, food, your car, even prescription medications and health care—because you *feel* like you have to pay them first. You have to "meet your obligations" in order to maintain your pride and dignity.

#3 They love your responsible nature. The more you blame yourself for "getting yourself into this mess" the less likely you are to blame your creditors. They love it when you say, "This is ALL my fault." Because as long as you're pointing the finger at yourself, you're not thinking about the late charges and the skyrocketing interest rates they're charging you in an effort not *just* to make money but *to keep you exactly where you are*: Under...Their...Control.

#4 They know it's NOT "all your fault." Anyone in the lending business knows that people fall on hard times. They know all about medical bills, divorce, and losing jobs. After all, that's why our country has bankruptcy laws in the first place. Your creditors know that you would pay your bills if you could. They *know* that. So what does it mean when they send collection companies after you demanding to be paid? It means they know you're probably in trouble and they *just don't care*. They just want to collect as much as possible from you before you drown in debt and declare bankruptcy.

#5 Your creditors think you're a sucker. When you signed up for your credit cards or bought your home, did you sit down and read the *entire* agreement? You know, the one in very tiny print that talks about late fees, calling your loan early when you miss payments, raising your credit card rates to 26% when you pay late? Of course not! Almost no one does! Don't you think your creditors know that? Don't you think they're taking advantage of the fact that you don't really know all the consequences of a couple late payments? They know it alright...and they LOVE the fact that you don't.

The trouble with your creditors is that they love and care about you for ALL the wrong reasons.

They love and care for you the way a farmer loves his Thanksgiving turkey. It's all about what they can get from you in the end.

So if you've convinced yourself that you absolutely must do the "right thing", it's time to realize who you're dealing with and ask yourself what the "right thing" really is for you and for your family.

The Top 10 Secrets Your Creditors Don't Want YOU to Know

As you've learned, your creditors would like to keep you right where you are: in debt up to your eyeballs with no apparent way out. By keeping you under their control they not only make money, they wield financial and emotional control over you, over your assets, and even over those you love.

But in order to keep you in your current position, they have to completely ignore the secrets that, if known, could lead to your freedom. Think about it. Have any of the debt collectors who contact you every day offered *any other option* other than paying your bills? Of course not!

They won't mention any of the following secrets because your creditors know that as soon as YOU know what the secrets are, their plans to take you for all your worth fall apart.

The Top 10 Bankruptcy Secrets Your Creditors Don't Want You to Know is designed to give you power over your creditors. When you know the TRUTH about what your options are, you'll never be under your creditors' control again.

I'll cover each secret in depth in the following chapters. But consider the fact that knowing just ONE of these 10 Secrets can thwart your creditors' devious plans entirely!

Secret #1: Bankruptcy Can Eliminate Your Debts OR Help You Pay Them Off

Imagine being able to be relieved of your debts…without selling yourself or your family into slavery. Bankruptcy gives you the opportunity to eliminate debts or even to pay them off by developing a payment plan that works for you on your family.

Secret #2: Filing Bankruptcy Will STOP the Debt Collection Calls

Has anyone who called you on the phone ever mentioned that all you have to do to get them to stop calling is to file bankruptcy? That's right. As soon as you file, they are prohibited *by law* from contacting you.

Secret #3: Bankruptcy Can STOP Foreclosure

If someone from the bank is calling about the fact that you're behind on your mortgage payments, try asking them how you can stop the foreclosure proceedings. Most likely they'll tell you to "bring your mortgage payments current." What they won't tell you is to file for bankruptcy because bankruptcy can stop the foreclosure *and help you get current on your payments*.

Secret #4: You Won't "Lose Everything"

Your creditors won't tell you the truth about bankruptcy because they like you to think that you'll lose everything. As long as you're terrified of losing everything, you'll keep making payments and doing your best to keep everything. The fact is, you won't lose everything. All you have to gain is freedom…from *them*.

Secret #5: You Will Still Be Able to Purchase a Home or a Car

Like your fear of losing everything, your creditors love hiding this secret too. They want you to think you'll lose everything AND they want you to think *that you'll NEVER be able to get it back again.* Fear of loss on this scale paralyzes you...and keeps you sacrificing everything to keep making payments.

Secret #6: You Don't Have to Be Out of Work to File Bankruptcy

While it certainly helps, you don't have to be out of work to file bankruptcy. Don't let anyone tell you otherwise. You only need to show that your debts exceed your expenses and that you can't afford to pay. So don't go quitting your job or getting yourself fired. You don't have to be out of work to file bankruptcy.

Secret #7: Even High-Income Earners Can Qualify for Bankruptcy

It's easy for others to look at you, especially if you have a high income, and think that you can afford everything. But we all know that the more you earn the more you spend. Don't be tricked into believing that as a high income earner you can't file bankruptcy and find relief. You can.

Secret #8: Credit Counselors are NOT Your Friends

If you are considering credit counseling, think again. Getting involved with the wrong organization can ruin your credit and drain your financial resources.

Secret #9: You Can File Bankruptcy More Than Once

Depending on the timing of your previous bankruptcy (if you have one or more), you may be eligible to file again now. Don't let your creditors make you believe there's only one "Get Out of Jail Free" card in the deck. If you need relief again, it is possible to file more than once.

Secret #10: You Don't Need an Attorney to File Bankruptcy

You may be shocked that as an attorney I'm telling you that you might not need one. But the point of this book is to reveal secrets…not hide them! If you have a very simple Chapter 7 bankruptcy, you may be able to file without the help of an attorney.

I share these secrets to give you hope. You don't have to believe everything you hear. And your options to regain your financial freedom are more easily obtainable than you might think.

Keep reading to learn about the details of each of the 10 secrets. And, as always, if you have questions or need assistance, I am at your service.

Secret #1:
Bankruptcy Can Eliminate Your Debts OR Help You Pay Them Off

Many people assume there's only one type of bankruptcy: the one that eliminates all your debts. That's a BIG reason people say things like, "I would *never* declare bankruptcy!" It just doesn't seem to be the responsible thing to do. Right?

What most people don't know is that there are TWO types of bankruptcy available to individuals:

Chapter 7 Bankruptcy lets you eliminate most of your debts (with a few exceptions) in order to get a fresh financial start in life.

Chapter 13 Bankruptcy lets you restructure your debts. This may eliminate *some* debt. But the primary goal is to renegotiate your existing debts so they are easier for you to pay off. Chapter 13 can also help you stop foreclosure and save your home by developing a plan that allows you to catch up on missed payments.

So if you're still determined to pay your debts in full AND you can't see a way to ever accomplish that goal, this may be just the secret you need to know!

Understanding the Two Types of Bankruptcy

These two types of bankruptcy are intended to achieve *very* different goals. Before taking action it is important to understand what you want to achieve and which type of bankruptcy is right for you.

Here is a quick summary of each type of bankruptcy and how each one can help you achieve specific goals in your financial life.

Chapter 7 Bankruptcy

Chapter 7 bankruptcy is the most common type of bankruptcy for consumers. Its liquidation feature is designed to eliminate debts and give you a fresh start.

What Chapter 7 Achieves. It is most commonly used to discharge credit card debts, deficiency balances on cars and homes, judgments and some taxes.

What You Must Disclose. In both types of bankruptcy, you must disclose all your assets and liabilities. Hiding assets in bankruptcy is a federal crime.

Debts It Will Not Discharge. It won't discharge child support, alimony, student loans or taxes less than three years old.

What Happens to Your Home. With regard to your home, a Chapter 7 bankruptcy cancels all the debt secured by your home including first mortgages and home equity loans. It may also cancel taxes associated with your home. With Chapter 7, you will most likely lose your home.

How Long It Takes. Like Chapter 13 bankruptcy, an automatic stay begins when you file Chapter 7 bankruptcy. After filing, a Chapter 7 bankruptcy takes three to four months to get a discharge.

How You Qualify. Depending on your income level, you may not qualify to file a Chapter 7 bankruptcy. The Bankruptcy Abuse Prevention and Consumer Protection Act of 2005 provides that anyone whose average gross income for the six-month period before the bankruptcy filing exceeds the state median income for the same sized household is ineligible to file Chapter 7 bankruptcy. Eligibility is determined by "means testing"—a formula applied to determine whether you have the "means" to pay your existing debts or not. **Before you assume you are not eligible for Chapter 7 bankruptcy, please consult an attorney who can make this determination for you. The result often depends on how you do the math.**

Chapter 13 Bankruptcy

Chapter 13 bankruptcy is commonly referred to as "reorganization". Its main use is to keep a house with a mortgage when you are behind in payments. It is also used when you have extra income and can afford to pay back some debts if the payment plan is structured favorably.

What Chapter 13 Achieves. Chapter 13 allows you to keep your home and most of your assets. A "plan of reorganization" must be filed with the court. The plan tells the Trustee (who holds and controls your assets during bankruptcy proceedings) how to pay your creditors during the reorganization. Chapter 13 may also eliminate second and third mortgages by recategorizing them as unsecured debt. However, this depends on your current amount of debt in comparison to the value of your home and what the home equity loans were used for.

What You Must Disclose. In both types of bankruptcy, you must disclose all your assets and liabilities. Hiding assets in bankruptcy is a federal crime.

Debts It Will Not Discharge. A Chapter 13 bankruptcy will restructure the terms of your mortgage rather than discharging the loan. It won't discharge child support, alimony, student loans or taxes less than three years old.

What Happens to Your Home. The intention of Chapter 13 bankruptcy is to help you keep your home. It helps you set up a plan to pay back the payment you've missed over a designated period of time while making current payments at the same time. It also helps you become current with other creditors with liens against assets you would like to keep. Assets associated with debts you would like to discharge during the bankruptcy can be liquidated by the court.

How Long It Takes. An automatic stay begins when you file Chapter 13 bankruptcy. After filing, a Chapter 13 bankruptcy takes three to five years to get a discharge, depending on the status of the debts you have agreed to repay.

How You Qualify. To file Chapter 13 as an individual, you must be able to demonstrate to the courts that after certain debts are discharged that you will still have sufficient disposable income to meet the requirements of the payment plan set up by the court. That is the primary requirement. Businesses cannot file Chapter 13 bankruptcy but business owners can file Chapter 13 as individuals.

Success Story: Chapter 7 Bankruptcy

Mr. and Mrs. P. were retired. Mr. P. made $1,500/month from his military pension. Mrs. P. made $3,000 from her pension as a school teacher. They owned a home worth $240,000 that had a mortgage owed of $320,000. They had combined credit card debt and some medical bills of around $18,000. They filed a Chapter 7 bankruptcy, surrendering the house back to the mortgage company. They discharged (aka eliminated) their credit card debt and medical bills. They moved into a house in the same neighborhood as their old house, paying half as much in rent as they were paying on their mortgage.

Success Story: Chapter 13 Bankruptcy

Mrs. R. had a mortgage of $80,000 on her house worth $90,000. She got behind three months because of a layoff from her job. Her monthly payments were $850/month, including taxes and insurance.

The mortgage company accelerated her note and started a foreclosure. Adding up attorney fees plus missed payments, Mrs. R. needed $4,150 to reinstate her mortgage. She filed a Chapter 13 bankruptcy that stopped the foreclosure. It cost her a lot less than the $4,150 she needed to bring the mortgage current. The payment plan we negotiated with the court—in order to pay off the $4,150 *plus* $6,500 in credit card debt—was only $250 per month. She was able to keep her home and resume making her normal mortgage payment.

Secret #2: Filing Bankruptcy Will STOP the Debt Collection Calls

Do you feel a rush of anxiety every time the phone rings? Are you worried that every call may be just one more creditor trying to collect from you? Have you stopped answering the phone altogether...or even unplugged it...because you just can't handle the stress anymore?

Then here's some good news...

According to federal law, once you file for bankruptcy, your attorney becomes your legal representative. Rather than contacting you directly, all your collectors *must* deal directly with your attorney.

All attempts to collect from you directly—by mail, by phone, or in any other way—must stop because of something called an "automatic stay." (To learn more about your rights in relation to debt collectors, visit the Federal Trade Commission's Consumer Information site at www.consumer.ftc.gov/articles/0149-debt-collection.)

An automatic stay prohibits nearly every kind of collection activity, including:

- Legal action
- Garnishment of your wages
- Contact by phone
- Contact by mail

While the automatic stay may not stop criminal proceedings, evictions, or some issues related to collecting child support, it *will* stop the calls right away.

If for some reason creditors do continue to contact you, they are in violation of the automatic stay. All you need to do is inform them that you have filed bankruptcy and they should immediately stop all collection actions in order to correct their violation.

If creditors continue to call after having been informed of your bankruptcy filing, you can notify the bankruptcy court. The court will take the matter from there and may even sanction the collection agency, depending on whether the violation was a willful act or an honest mistake.

Don't fall prey to debt collectors who may not be completely honest about your rights under the law and when or how much you must pay.

Success Story: Stopping the Calls

Sean P. got his Master's Degree. He took out $60,000 in student loan debts. He got married then two children. He had managed to keep things going financially for years by supplementing his income with credit card debt. As time went on, he got to the point where he couldn't afford to pay his minimum payments anymore. He had reached his limit on credit cards and they weren't going down.

Sean was getting phone calls from bill collectors almost daily. He was overwhelmed with debt and headed toward depression. He filed for bankruptcy and got a fresh start. He felt relieved and grateful. He told me, "I should have filed for bankruptcy two years ago." He worked out a repayment plan with the student loans (since they were not dischargeable) and was able to live comfortably, staying up to date on all his payments.

Are Debt Collectors Getting You Down?

If you're receiving regular calls from creditors and are considering bankruptcy, please call to schedule a FREE consultation. There is no obligation to file bankruptcy. A consultation will help you get clear about your options and whether bankruptcy is something you should consider.

To schedule your complimentary consultation, please call my office at:

(314) 968-1313

Secret #3: Bankruptcy Can STOP Foreclosure

If you have mounting debt and collectors are calling, it's likely that you're also behind on your mortgage payments. One missed payment is hard to catch up on. But once you miss three or four, it's almost too late. The mortgage company accelerates your mortgage and the foreclosure process begins.

Even if the events that caused you to miss payments are behind you, the mortgage company won't accept your payments because the note has been accelerated (meaning you now owe the *entire balance* due on your loan, plus penalties and late fees, not just the payments you've missed).

The possibility of losing your home plus the stress of creditors calling every day is beyond stressful. It can literally make you sick. According to a recent study, homeowners in foreclosure are more prone to depression and are more likely to skip doctor visits and go without prescription medication.[5]

If you're like most people facing foreclosure, you probably got behind on your payments for good reasons:

- Job loss
- Loss of income
- Illness

---

[5] Robert Wood Johnson Foundation. "Foreclosure Process Takes Toll on Physical, Mental Health". www.rwjf.org/en/about-rwjf/newsroom/newsroom-content/2011/10/foreclosure-process-takes-toll-on-physical-mental-health.html

- Medical expenses
- Divorce
- Helping a family member

Foreclosure is often a symptom of general financial problems in personal or family life that make saving a home from foreclosure unlikely to happen without outside help from family, friends or legal action like bankruptcy.

I've never seen anyone come up with the entire amount of the mortgage to stop a foreclosure. But I have seen many people afford the attorney's fees it takes to file bankruptcy and save their home.

The least expensive, easiest and most successful way to stop a foreclosure in Missouri is to file bankruptcy. Bankruptcy automatically stops the foreclosure and allows you to keep your home (if you can afford the payment plan).

Here's how it works…

Delaying Foreclosure with the Automatic Stay

When you file bankruptcy—either Chapter 7 or Chapter 13—an "automatic stay" goes into effect. This means your creditors are temporarily prohibited from collecting debts from you. Not only can they not actively pursue collection, they aren't even allowed to contact you by phone or by mail.

However, the automatic stay doesn't last forever.

If your home is scheduled for foreclosure and you file a Chapter 7 or Chapter 13 bankruptcy, you should end up with about three to four months to work things out.

But the automatic stay doesn't guarantee you will be able to save your home. Saving your home depends on two things: the type of bankruptcy you file and your financial capabilities.

Chapter 7 Bankruptcy and Foreclosure

Chapter 7 bankruptcy is designed to discharge (eliminate) your debts. This includes the mortgage against your home. You should only file Chapter 7 bankruptcy if your intention is to give your home back to the bank and find another place to live. The automatic stay that accompanies Chapter 7 bankruptcy buys you time to find a new home. This may be your best option if you are sure you won't be able to afford mortgage payments plus the additional cost of repaying payments you have missed. It may be better to let the home go to the bank and find some place more affordable to live.

If you are willing to let your home go, Chapter 7 bankruptcy eliminates your mortgage debt entirely. You will be free from the debt and the monthly payments. This should increase your disposable income.

Chapter 13 Bankruptcy and Foreclosure

While Chapter 7 eliminates your debts, Chapter 13 "restructures" them. Chapter 13 gives you the opportunity to negotiate both debts and payments with your creditors. This often results in a payment plan that allows you to repay your debts (some in part and some in full) over a specified course of time and often on a lower payment schedule. Repayment plans typically range from three to five years.

In order to keep your home, you will have to be able to afford mortgage payments *plus* the additional amount of the "catch up" payments. Of course, the court won't just take your word for it. You will need to provide financial evidence showing that after a restructuring of your debts and assets that you will have enough disposable income to make the payments.

Success Story: Stopping Foreclosure

C.P. worked for the U.S. Postal Service. Her son got into some difficulty with the law and she helped him out by giving him some money. As a result, C.P. fell behind on her mortgage payments and couldn't get caught back up. The mortgage company scheduled her home for foreclosure in 20 days. She tried everything to catch up the mortgage, asking everyone she knew for money. Time was running out fast. She contacted me and filed a Chapter 13 bankruptcy. The foreclosure was stopped and C.P. kept her home. She makes her mortgage payments her first priority now.

Do You Want to Stop Your Foreclosure?

If you would like to determine whether or not bankruptcy can help you save your home, please call to schedule a complimentary consultation today.

To schedule an appointment, please call:
(314) 968-1313

Secret #4: You Won't "Lose Everything"

Bankruptcy is designed to give good people who have had bad things happen to them a fresh start. But what most people want is a fresh start without having to start completely from scratch. Because of this, a major concern about filing bankruptcy is that you will "lose everything".

A fresh start under Missouri law is defined by exemptions. Exemptions outline the types of property and possessions that are necessary to have a fresh start without having to start over completely.

Each state has the option to use federal exemptions or to create its own exemptions. Missouri has chosen to create its own exemptions and these exemptions will determine what property you may keep after your bankruptcy has been discharged (aka completed).

A Fresh Start vs. A Head Start

According to Missouri exemptions, it is reasonable to exempt enough property to provide shelter, furnish that shelter, clothe yourself and your family members, have transportation and have a retirement account. So you will be able to keep most, if not all, of your property when you file for bankruptcy. When some property that you want to keep is not exempt from the bankruptcy, you can still keep it by repaying your creditors the difference between the exempt amount and the non-exempt amount. (This is one of the uses of a Chapter 13 reorganization plan.)

For example, Missouri exemptions protect up to $3,000 equity in a vehicle. If you own a car debt-free that is worth $4,500, you can arrange to pay the $1,500 of non-exempt value so that you can keep the car.

Bankruptcy is designed to give you a fresh start, but not a head start. That's one of the reasons that student loan debt is not dischargeable. Statistics show that the more education someone gets, the more income they will earn over their lifetime. Congress has decided that it's too much of a head start to give people who get a higher education the ability to eliminate student loan debt via bankruptcy.

Success Story: Getting a Fresh Start

Mr. R. R. worked in the medical industry for 20 years. He owned his house with a mortgage and two vehicles: a beat up truck worth about $600 and an everyday driver car worth about $3,500. Both cars were paid for. His house had about $20,000 worth of equity. He had the normal amount of furniture, clothing and jewelry. He got burned out from working around sick and dying people all the time. He felt he had to take a break from the medical industry. So he took a job in retail where his income dropped, nearly in half. He couldn't afford his credit card debts any longer and fell behind on his payments. He filed a Chapter 7 bankruptcy and got the relief he needed. He also got to keep all of his property. He got the fresh start he needed.

How Much Will You Get to Keep?

Are you considering bankruptcy but concerned about losing property or assets? Why not come in for a free consultation? We can discuss your assets and determine what you would like be able to keep and what might likely be taken by the court.

To schedule an appointment, please call:

(314) 968-1313

Secret #5:
You Will Still Be Able to Purchase a Home or a Car

If you've asked anyone about bankruptcy, you've probably heard that it will "ruin your credit score" and that "you'll never be able to get credit again". Hogwash!

It is true that bankruptcy affects your credit score. Bankruptcy is public record and it stays on your credit report for seven to ten years. However, that doesn't mean it stops you from getting new credit or buying a new home or car after your bankruptcy is discharged.

Once a discharge is granted, you will be debt-free, with the exception of student loans, child support, alimony, and taxes less than three years old. Usually this means there is money left over in your budget.

Creditors love to see extra spending money. (And, of course, they would love to get their hands on it too!) To them, extra spending money means you can afford to repay newly incurred debts. Because they profit by lending money, they are always on the lookout for new prospects (like you) to lend money to. Who better to lend money to than someone who has just come out of bankruptcy, has no debt, has extra spending money, and who hopefully learned their lesson about paying their bills on time?

Rather than a shortage of credit after bankruptcy, credit card offers and automobile offers will flood your mailbox. You will have many new choices to make regarding new credit. (One of which might be to avoid credit card debt altogether.)

The key after bankruptcy is to repay any new credit you obtain *on time*. By paying back any new credit you get, you may qualify for a mortgage under current FHA/VA guidelines within one to two years.

Another reason it's easy to incur new debt after bankruptcy is that creditors know you can only get one bankruptcy discharge (Chapter 7) every eight years. That means if you should default on any newly incurred debt, the creditor has plenty of time to collect it from you in other ways.

In short, if you're worried that bankruptcy will ruin your chances of ever accessing credit again...don't. You'll have all the credit you need.

What About My Credit Score?

If you're late or behind in payments, chances are that you've already damaged your credit score.

Here's what MyFico.com has to say in answer to this question:[6]

> *A bankruptcy will always be considered a very negative event by your FICO® score. How much of an impact it will have on your score will depend on your entire credit profile. For example, someone that had spotless credit and a very high FICO score could expect a huge drop in their score. On the other hand, someone with many negative items already listed on their credit report might only see a modest drop in their score. Another thing to note is that the more accounts included in the bankruptcy filing, the more of an impact on your score.*

Credit scores are a big determinant creditors use when deciding whether or not to lend money, and at what rates to lend. After you get a discharge in bankruptcy, generally speaking, within one year

---

[6] http://www.myfico.com/crediteducation/questions/bankruptcy-fico-score.aspx

your credit may go back up 100 points or more. The key factor in raising your credit score is to never be 30 days late on any debts after bankruptcy. Pay back any new debts on time or early to build credit scores even faster.

Success Story: Credit to Buy a Home

Mr. J.D. is a disabled police officer. His wife is a teacher. They used to own a house in South County St. Louis. It was worth $300,000 before 2008 and they owed $280,000. After 2008, the value of the house went down to $210,000. They filed a Chapter 7 bankruptcy. After the discharge, they rented a house with an option to buy. Two years after the bankruptcy, they qualified for an FHA mortgage and bought the house they were renting. Without the stress of the debt they had before the bankruptcy, they were able to enjoy life much better. During the two years before purchasing the home, they saved up money for the down payment, which was much easier since they were debt free.

Success Story: Buying a Used Car

D.Z. filed a Chapter 7 bankruptcy. He and his wife both worked. They had three children together. Expenses always seemed to exceed their incomes. They supplemented their incomes for years with credit card purchases. It got to the point where they couldn't afford to raise their family any longer and repay old debts. They filed a Chapter 7 bankruptcy and discharged over $30,000 in credit card debts. The day after receiving a discharge, they were able to purchase a $10,000 used car from a local dealer. They put $500 down and their monthly payments were $300. That's how easy it is to get new credit after bankruptcy.

Secret #6:
You Don't Have to Be Out of Work to File Bankruptcy

You've probably figured this out by now, but you don't need to be out of work to file bankruptcy. The only requirement is proof that your contractual expenses—anything that you've agreed in writing to be responsible for—exceed your income or your ability to pay.

For Chapter 7 bankruptcy, you do need to qualify by passing something called the "means test". This test determines, based on your financial information, whether or not you have the "means" to pay your debts. If you don't have the means to pay, you can declare bankruptcy.

Taking the Means Test

Whether or not you are required to take the means test in order to qualify for a Chapter 7 bankruptcy depends on your income. If your household income is below the median income for the same size household in the State of Missouri, you don't need to take the means test.

If your income exceeds the median income for the same size household in Missouri, you will need to take and pass the means test in order to qualify to file Chapter 7 bankruptcy.

The means test takes your average monthly income and subtracts your expenses. It also compares some of your expenses to IRS standards to determine whether they are reasonable or not. Unfortunately, the means test seems to favor people will big mortgages, car payments and credit card debt.

Being over the median doesn't mean you can't file bankruptcy. It just means you'll need the help of an attorney to crunch the numbers and help you qualify.

NOTE: You do not need to pass any tests in order to file Chapter 13 bankruptcy.

Success Story: Passing the Means Test

Mr. Courtney E. filed a Chapter 7 Bankruptcy in 2012. He had listed an expense of $1,500 per month in court ordered payments on his Means Test in order to qualify for a Chapter 7 bankruptcy. The Office of the United States Trustee reviewed his case for abuse. We advised Mr. E. of exactly what was needed in order to prove his expense. The Trustee accepted the proof he provided per our advice and Mr. E. received his discharge.

Worried About Passing the Means Test?

Many people hesitate to come in for a consultation because they think they must be ready to file bankruptcy right away. I understand what a difficult decision bankruptcy really is. Sometimes the best thing you can do is gather *more* information to help you make the *best* decision possible. So why not come in to discuss your financial situation, determine whether you can pass the means test, and then see where you'd like to go from there.

To schedule a complimentary consultation, please call:

(314) 968-1313

IMPORTANT: Be sure to mention you'd like to discuss means testing. There may be financial information you will need to bring with you to the appointment.

Secret #7: Even High-Income Earners Can Qualify for Bankruptcy

You've probably heard the saying, "You spend what you earn." And the more people earn, the more they tend to spend. If you're looking at bankruptcy, you are spending *more* than you earn.

So when it comes to bankruptcy, it doesn't really matter if you're rich, poor or somewhere in between. What matters is that you've taken on debt—by buying things you want—and now you find yourself unable to pay what you owe.

Since that's the situation that drives people into bankruptcy, it should be no surprise that high-income earners often find it easiest to qualify for bankruptcy. Even when it comes to means testing, people with big mortgages, car payments and credit card balances often find it easiest to qualify—even easier than middle class folks renting houses and driving paid off cars. Why is it easier to qualify?

The more debt you take on, the more likely you are to end up in bankruptcy!

What About Means Testing?

If you want to discharge your debts, you're likely wondering how you can pass the means test when, as a high income earner, you're way above the median income for your state.

Good question.

Being over the median income doesn't mean you can't file a Chapter 7 bankruptcy. It just means you need a good attorney who can help you crunch the numbers and qualify.

If you do qualify to file, your next challenge will be to convince the judge of the following:

- You're acting in good faith and really *do* need a discharge of debts
- Your daily living expenses are reasonable

And if you happen to be a business owner and 51% or more of your debts are business related, you can file a Chapter 7 bankruptcy regardless of your disposable income. You'll definitely want to work with an experienced bankruptcy attorney to ensure that the debts you consider "business debts" meet the court's criteria in order for you to file a Chapter 7 case without taking the means test.

If for some reason you can't qualify to file Chapter 7, you will still be eligible to file Chapter 13 if you can demonstrate sufficient disposable income to fund the repayment plan.

Success Story: High Income Earners File Chapter 13 Bankruptcy

Mrs. Yvonne M. earned $101,000 in 2013. She had applied for a loan modification on her mortgage that had a payment of $3,432/mo. She had a car payment of $650/mo. She was married and had two minor children living with her. Her husband's income was $42,000/yr. When she applied for the loan modification her mortgage company told her to stop making her mortgage payments. They turned her down for the loan modification after taking 4 months, and requesting paperwork after paperwork. By the time the mortgage company decided not to do a loan modification they demanded $14,532 to bring her mortgage current. Mrs. M. had not saved the mortgage payments, but rather had used the money to pay other debts. She filed a Chapter 13 bankruptcy and was able to catch up her mortgage payments and consolidate her other debts into one affordable payment.

Success Story: High Income Earners File Chapter 7 Bankruptcy

Mr. and Mrs. C.S. both had good paying jobs. They had even managed to buy a rental property for an investment. But Mr. C.S. was a mortgage banker. When the Great Recession of 2008 hit, it devastated his industry and his income. To make matters worse, a flood ruined their investment property. They filed a claim with their insurance company but they refused to pay for the damaged citing that floods are not covered.

Mr. and Mrs. C.S. retained an attorney to fight the insurance company, but it was costing more money than they could afford to pay. So they decided to file for bankruptcy. They surrendered their investment property and eliminated $55,000 in credit card debt while keeping their house and cars. They got the fresh start they needed.

Success Story: Discharging Business Debts

Mr. and Mrs. Ron and Vicki K. owned and operated a Travel Company. Ron did the sales and Vicki did the bookkeeping and the operations. The business was incorporated as an LLC, but personal guarantees were also required by their creditors. After about 5 years of operating the business sales began to slow down, the airlines changed the fees required, and the business began to lose money.

Rather than continue to take money out of his 401k which had about $250,000, Ron and Vicki K. decided to close down the business. All the business assets were listed as well as all the business debts. They got a discharge and were able to keep their 401k in full, as well as discharge all the business debts, over $105,000 in total.

What Type of Bankruptcy Can You File?

If you're still wondering which type(s) of bankruptcy you can qualify for, it's likely that you need some help crunching the numbers. Please compile a list of assets and debts and then come in for a visit. We'll run the numbers together and determine exactly what your options are.

To schedule a complimentary consultation, please call:

(314) 968-1313

IMPORTANT: Be sure to mention that you want to figure out what type of bankruptcy you can file. You will be asked to bring specific information with you to your appointment.

Secret #8: Credit Counselors are NOT Your Friends

Many people think it's best to try credit counseling before they investigate bankruptcy. But I'm here to tell you that many of these companies are not acting in your best interest.

Many credit counseling agencies are paid—and in some cases managed—by credit card companies. If they are not acting in the interest of the credit card companies, they will fight against them while destroying your credit at the same time.

According to an article by financial guru Dave Ramsey:

> "Some of these 'counseling' companies withhold credit card payments until the account is three to six months past due. Then, they contact the lender and negotiate to settle the bad debt....That's how they get negotiated discounts on credit card debt. Card companies don't settle on your debts when your payments are on time. These services are always a bad idea, and sometimes they're a complete scam."[7]

Dave Ramsey isn't the only one leery of credit counselors. The federal government has its own opinion.

---

[7] http://www.cbn.com/finance/ramsey041410.aspx

What the U.S. Government Says About Credit Counselors and Bankruptcy

You're probably wondering whether, as a bankruptcy attorney, I might steer you away from credit counselors just so I can get your business. That's a perfectly legitimate concern. And just so you can see I'm not the only one singing this tune, here are just a few quotes from our own U.S. Federal Trade Commission's website:[8]

About Credit Counseling

> "Most reputable credit counselors are non-profit and offer services at local offices, online, or on the phone. If possible, find an organization that offers in-person counseling. Many universities, military bases, credit unions, housing authorities, and branches of the U.S. Cooperative Extension Service operate non-profit credit counseling programs. Your financial institution, local consumer protection agency, and friends and family also may be good sources of information and referrals.

> "But be aware that 'non-profit' status doesn't guarantee that services are free, affordable, or even legitimate. In fact, some credit counseling organizations charge high fees, which they may hide; others might urge their clients to make 'voluntary' contributions that can cause more debt."

About Bankruptcy and Mandatory Credit Counseling

> "**Bankruptcy**. Declaring bankruptcy has serious consequences, including lowering your credit score, but credit counselors and other experts say that in some cases, it may make the most sense. Filing for bankruptcy under Chapter 13 allows people with a steady income to keep property, like a mortgaged house or a car, that they might otherwise lose through the Chapter 7

---

[8] http://www.consumer.ftc.gov/articles/0153-choosing-credit-counselor

bankruptcy process. In Chapter 13, the court approves a repayment plan that allows you to pay off your debts over a three to five year period, without surrendering any property. After you have made all the payments under the plan, your debts are discharged. As part of the Chapter 13 process, you will have to pay a lawyer, and you must get credit counseling from a government-approved organization within six months before you file for any bankruptcy relief.

"You can find a state-by-state list of government-approved organizations at the U.S. Trustee Program, the organization within the U.S. Department of Justice that supervises bankruptcy cases and trustees."

About Choosing an Organization for Mandatory Credit Counseling

Once you've got a list of counseling agencies you might do business with, check each one out with your state Attorney General and local consumer protection agency. They can tell you if consumers have filed complaints about any one of them. (If there are no complaints about them, don't consider it a guarantee that they're legitimate.) The United States Trustee Program also keeps a list of credit counseling agencies approved to provide pre-bankruptcy counseling. After you've done your background investigation, you will want to interview the final "candidates."

Here are some questions to ask to help you find the best counselor for you.

- **What services do you offer?** Look for an organization that offers a range of services, including budget counseling, and savings and debt management classes. Avoid organizations that push a debt management plan (DMP) as your only option before they spend a significant amount of time analyzing your financial situation.

- **Do you offer information?** Are educational materials available for free? Avoid organizations that charge for information.

- **In addition to helping me solve my immediate problem, will you help me develop a plan for avoiding problems in the future?**

- **What are your fees?** Are there set-up and/or monthly fees? Get a specific price quote in writing.

- **What if I can't afford to pay your fees or make contributions?** If an organization won't help you because you can't afford to pay, look elsewhere for help.

- **Will I have a formal written agreement or contract with you?** Don't sign anything without reading it first. Make sure all verbal promises are in writing.

- **Are you licensed to offer your services in my state?**

- **What are the qualifications of your counselors?** Are they accredited or certified by an outside organization? If so, by whom? If not, how are they trained? Try to use an organization whose counselors are trained by a non-affiliated party.

- **What assurance do I have that information about me (including my address, phone number, and financial information) will be kept confidential and secure?**

- **How are your employees paid?** Are they paid more if I sign up for certain services, if I pay a fee, or if I make a contribution to your organization? If the answer is yes, consider it a red flag and go elsewhere for help.

Even if you decide to declare bankruptcy, you'll still need a credit counselor at some point. Just be sure to select one that is reputable, that won't ruin your credit and that won't take you for a ride.

Success Story: Completing Required Credit Counseling in ONE Day

Under the current laws, everyone who files for bankruptcy must complete a pre-bankruptcy credit counseling course. The charge for the counseling ranges from $15-$60 depending on which agency you use. Mr. Christian M. needed to file his bankruptcy the same day he came into my office. We completed all his schedules, statements, and means test requirements, but he still needed the certificate of credit counseling before he could file his case. We gave him a postcard from one of our recommended credit counseling agencies and he was able to complete the course on-line in about an hour. It cost him $15 which he paid with a pre-paid debit card. The credit counseling agency emailed us the certificate and we were able to file his case the same day. That stopped a creditor from garnishing his paycheck the next day.

Would You Like a Referral to a Credit Counselor?

For a list of Ridings Law Approved credit counseling agencies, please call:

(314) 968-1313

Secret #9:
You Can File Bankruptcy More Than Once

Sometimes you just have a string of bad luck. Instead of weathering the trials of one stressful experience, they hit you in succession.

Sometimes financial problems lead to bankruptcy. The financial stress contributes to marital problems that lead to divorce. Then, the hardships of supporting two households, combined with the emotional strain and other unexpected crises, put you right back where you were when you filed bankruptcy the *first* time!

Depending on the type of bankruptcy you've filed in the past and how long it's been since your bankruptcy was discharged, you may be able to file more than once, if necessary.

How Often Can You File Bankruptcy?
When you can file bankruptcy and the type of bankruptcy you can file depends on the type of bankruptcy you have filed before.

Here are some of the rules...

Chapter 7 Filing. If you want to file a Chapter 7 bankruptcy, you can typically file a new case and receive a discharge:

- Eight years after filing a previous Chapter 7 bankruptcy
- Six years after filing a previous Chapter 13 bankruptcy

Chapter 13 Filing. If you want to file a Chapter 13 bankruptcy, you can typically file a new case and receive a discharge:

- Four years after filing a previous Chapter 7 bankruptcy
- Two years after filing a previous Chapter 13 bankruptcy

The rules may apply to you differently if you filed a bankruptcy case that was dismissed rather than discharged.

Changes to Automatic Stay on a Second Filing

One of the benefits to filing bankruptcy is the automatic stay that goes into effect immediately after filing your case. Traditionally, the automatic stay allows you three to four months in order to sort things out, even if your case doesn't end in a discharge.

However, if you have previously filed once for bankruptcy in the 12 months preceding your filing, the automatic stay only lasts for 30 days. If you've filed two times or more in the previous 12 months, you won't receive an automatic stay at all.

Success Story: Filing Bankruptcy More Than Once

Jack M. is an electrician and had worked with an IBEW Local Union for 16 years. He lost his job in January, 2014. He began to collect unemployment, but it was not enough to pay his mortgage and other household living expenses. He filed a Chapter 13 bankruptcy in April, 2014 to reorganize his debts and keep his property. He was still not back to work yet, but he was hopeful. Three months later, his case was dismissed for failure to make the agreed upon planned payments. He filed a Chapter 7 bankruptcy in July, 2014. In October, 2014 he received a discharge of all his debts. He just got another job, and filed another Chapter 13 later on in October, 2014. This is his second Chapter 13 and 3rd bankruptcy filing. He is able to keep his house and pay back the mortgage arrears inside his current Chapter 13 plan.

Find Out If You Can File Again

Are you wondering if you are eligible to file bankruptcy again?

Find out what your options are! Come in this week for a complimentary consultation.

To schedule a FREE consultation, please call:
(314) 968-1313

Secret #10:
You Don't Need an Attorney to File Bankruptcy

If you intend to file a Chapter 7 bankruptcy in order to have your debts discharged, it is possible to file your case without an attorney. This is referred to as filing "pro se". As a general rule, the simpler your case is, the easier it is to file pro se. If you have a complicated case or you intend to file a Chapter 13 bankruptcy, you will most certainly need the help of an attorney.

If you are thinking about representing yourself in your bankruptcy case, be advised that you will still be responsible for following all the rules governing bankruptcy. You won't receive any leniency for not knowing the law or the procedures just because you're taking a do-it-yourself approach to the process. And making mistakes will not only be frowned upon by the courts; it could have serious consequences.

Mistakes Often Made When Filing "Pro Se"

When you file pro se, you take full responsibility for any mistakes you make. Here are some of the most common mistakes to be aware of if you decide to file on your own:

- **Not listing all relevant debts.** If you accidently or intentionally leave out a debt when you submit your bankruptcy debt schedule, the debt will not be eliminated.

- **Not following procedures correctly.** Failing to file a required document at the appropriate time can result in your case being dismissed. A filing that results in a dismissal can prevent you from filing another bankruptcy and may eliminate certain protections if you do, such as the automatic stay.

- **Destroying or hiding property.** Hiding assets or eliminating them so you can qualify for bankruptcy may be a temptation (or even just seem like a good idea) when you are operating without the counsel of an attorney. Any such dishonesty, including falsifying records and lying about your debts and assets, is considered fraud. And because bankruptcy is filed in a federal court, this makes fraud a federal crime. In addition, the judge can elect *not* to discharge any of your debts.

- **Failing a bankruptcy audit.** Like tax filings, bankruptcy cases are randomly audited. Your case may also be audited if you file documents incorrectly and send up a red flag. If you have not submitted all the required information in an accurate, honest and complete manner, there may be consequences. If it is determined that you intentionally withheld information, your bankruptcy case could be dismissed and you could face fraud charges.

- **Not attending credit counseling.** As part of bankruptcy proceedings, you are required to attend credit counseling within 180 days before filing your case. You must also file a statement and a certificate of credit counseling to prove your attendance. Failing to do so could result in your case being dismissed. While credit counselors are often not your friends (especially when used *instead* of bankruptcy), dealing with them is a mandatory part of the bankruptcy process.

Even if you are thinking of filing on your own you will still benefit from the advice of an attorney. Please consider coming in for a consultation. Together we can determine the feasibility of your filing pro se and answer any questions you might have about the process.

Thinking of Filing Bankruptcy Yourself?

The process is complicated and requires huge attention to detail. If you would like an opinion as to whether you should file on your own or whether you really *should* hire an attorney, please call for an appointment today.

Call now to schedule your complimentary consultation:
(314) 968-1313

The Top 7 Reasons to Schedule a FREE Consultation with Ridings Law Firm

If you've read the book and not just skipped ahead, you know all the secrets about bankruptcy.

What will you do now?

The best thing you can do is schedule a FREE consultation!

Here's why:

1. **A free consultation is FREE.** It costs you absolutely nothing and you receive personalized advice from an attorney who files bankruptcies day in and day out.

2. **A free consultation is RELIEF.** There's honestly no better feeling than knowing you can be free from debt—or at least make it easier to bear. You'll walk away with a huge sense of relief knowing bankruptcy is an option for you.

3. **A free consultation is RECOMMENDED.** Any financial guru will tell you that getting reputable advice from an experienced attorney for free is a good thing.

4. **A free consultation is SMART.** The better educated you are about bankruptcy, the smarter decisions you can make about your financial situation.

5. **A free consultation means you're taking ACTION.** It's easy to be paralyzed by fear and uncertainty. Coming in for a consultation means you're taking action—however non-committal it may be—toward solving your financial problems.

6. **A free consultation outlines your OPTIONS.** You may not know which types of bankruptcy you can actually file for. Your free consultation will answer this question and more.

7. **A free consultation helps you DECIDE.** When you don't know what your options are or what the consequences of bankruptcy will be, how can you make any sort of decision? You can't! Your free consultation gives you the power to decide what to do next.

Schedule your FREE consultation today!

Call (314) 968-1313

About the Author

William H Ridings Jr, author of *The Top 10 Bankruptcy Secrets Your Creditors Don't Want You to Know*, holds a Juris Doctorate (J.D.) from St. Louis University School of Law and a B.S. in Finance from University of Missouri St. Louis. William has over 16 years of proven success in filing bankruptcy for over 4,000 clients and discharging over $100,000,000 in debts.

William graduated in 1990 with $60,000 in student loan debts. He has real life experience with dealing with unmanageable debts. After deferring and consolidating the federal student loan portion ($40,000) he tried to make the monthly payments but didn't have enough income…and so he defaulted. In 1998, Congress changed the bankruptcy laws so that student loan debt was not dischargeable. Also in 1998 William got into the Income Contingent Repayment Plan (ICRP) to pay back his federal student loan debt. Today, after paying back over $120,000, the balance on the student loans is still $126,000. This is because of capitalized interest and penalties and fines were added in. After being in the ICRP for 25 years the unpaid portion of the student loan will be forgiven.

William was a mortgage loan officer in 1997. He referred clients with poor credit scores or delinquent debts to other bankruptcy attorneys so that they could eliminate their debts and qualify for a mortgage loan in 1-2 years. His wife Linda suggested to him that he file the bankruptcy for his clients rather than refer them to other attorneys. So, that's what he did. Now he refers his clients to mortgage loan officers to qualify for mortgages 1-2 years after bankruptcy. Smart wife.

Contact Information:

William Ridings
2510 S. Brentwood Blvd, Ste 205
Brentwood, MO 63144
314-968-1313
www.RidingsLawFirm.com

www.ingramcontent.com/pod-product-compliance
Lightning Source LLC
Chambersburg PA
CBHW071817170526
45167CB00003B/1338